P9-AQK-831

MONEY SMART

EARNING

Dennis Brindell Fradin & Judith Bloom Fradin

MONEY SMART

EARNING

Dennis Brindell Fradin & Judith Bloom Fradin

Marshall Cavendish
Benchmark
New York

Website: www.marshallcavendish.us

This publication represents the opinions and views of the author based on Judith Bloom Fradin's and Dennis Brindell Fradin's personal experience, knowledge, and research. The information in this book serves as a general guide only. The author and publisher have used their best efforts in preparing this book and disclaim liability rising directly and indirectly from the use and application of this book.

Other Marshall Cavendish Offices:

Marshall Cavendish International (Asia) Private Limited, 1 New Industrial Road, Singapore 536196 • Marshall Cavendish International (Thailand) Co Ltd. 253 Asoke, 12th Flr, Sukhumvit 21 Road, Klongtoey Nua, Wattana, Bangkok 10110, Thailand • Marshall Cavendish (Malaysia) Sdn Bhd, Times Subang, Lot 46, Subang Hi-Tech Industrial Park, Batu Tiga, 40000 Shah Alam, Selangor Darul Ehsan, Malaysia

Marshall Cavendish is a trademark of Times Publishing Limited

All websites were available and accurate when this book was sent to press.

Library of Congress Cataloging-in-Publication Data
Fradin, Dennis Brindell.
Earning / by Dennis Brindell Fradin & Judith Bloom Fradin.
p. cm. — (Money smart)
Includes bibliographical references and index.
Summary: "Answers basic questions about earning money students ask when considering career choices and financial skills needed for adulthood"—Provided by publisher.
ISBN 978-1-60870-123-0
1. Vocational guidance—Juvenile literature. 2. Wages—Juvenile literature. I. Fradin, Judith Bloom. II. Title.
HF5381.2.F65 2011
331.702--dc22
2009045614

Editor: Deborah Grahame
Publisher: Michelle Bisson
Art Director: Anahid Hamparian
Series Designer: Kay Petronio
Photo research by Connie Gardner

Cover photo by Jeff Cadge/Getty Images

The photographs in this book are used by permission and through the courtesy of: *The Image Works:* akg-images, 6; *The Art Archive;* Charles R. Knight/NGS images, 9; Jean Vinchon Numsmatis, 10; *Getty Images:* Hulton Archive, 13; Pete Saloutos, 16; John Giustina, 19; Jetta Productions, 24; Nicolas Reynard, 27; Richard Drury, 28; Riser, 32, 52; AFP, 35, 40; Jim Boyle, 32; Holly Harris, 36; Stephen Derr, 46; Antonio Mo, 48; *PhotoEdit:* Felicia Martinez, 42.

Printed in Malaysia (T)

135642

CONTENTS

The mammoth, among other large mammals, may have been hunted to extinction during the Stone Age.

THE FIRST JOBS

ONE

The first human beings appeared on Earth more than a million years ago. Finding food was a full-time job for them. In fact, early human cultures spent so much time hunting animals and gathering plant foods that we call them hunter-gatherers. Once they ate the food in one place, they moved elsewhere in search of more. As a result, the hunter-gatherers had no permanent homes.

About 11,000 years ago, human beings developed a new way to get food: farming. They planted seeds, which grew into wheat, corn, and other crops. They tamed animals, which provided them with meat, milk, and eggs. Farming allowed people to put roots down in one place. Many families settled in areas where the soil was especially fertile and water was plentiful. These communities became the world's first towns.

The people of these early towns began to barter, or trade, with one another for goods and services they needed. Bartering allowed people to turn their special skills into jobs. For example, about ten thousand years ago, a prehistoric craftsman invented the first wooden plow. At about the same time, the practice of medicine began. We know this because scientists have found evidence of surgical procedures on prehistoric human fossils.

We do not know exactly how people began doing various jobs. As the word *prehistoric* means "before the time of writing," early humans did not leave us any words about their lives. But we can make a

WHAT CAN BE USED AS CURRENCY?

Anything can be used as currency as long as it is durable (lasts a long time), divisible (how do you divide a stone?), stores value (does not rot), universally accepted (lots of people are willing to use it), and won't be hoarded (the type of currency is valuable only as money).

Prehistoric people crafted canoes and oars to better pursue large mammals. They made spears to kill their prey.

reasonable guess about how it happened. For example, a skilled medicine woman or man treated a person who was ill. To pay for the treatment, the patient's family gave some wheat or a chicken to the prehistoric doctor. A farmer might have traded a cow for a plow.

Word spread that one person was a good healer and another person built plows to trade for other products. This was called specialization. It meant that a farmer could spend most of his time farming, the doctor could devote her life to healing people, and the builder could spend his time making plows. And so the first jobs were born.

This bronze spade coin was used as currency in China during the eighth to seventh centuries BCE.

THE INVENTION OF MONEY

Trading was not the answer for every transaction. A prehistoric doctor might not have wanted wheat or eggs every time she treated a sick person. A craftsman might not have wanted a cow as payment for every plow he made. People looked for new ways to pay for goods and services. A few thousand years ago, money was invented. The earliest known coins were created more than 2,600 years ago in the kingdom of Lydia in present-day Turkey. The first paper money was printed in China about 1,400 years ago.

The invention of money led to many new jobs. For example, people needed to keep their money in a safe place. This led to the creation

ODD MONEY

Over the centuries, people around the world have used some odd objects as money. The people of the Yap Islands in the Pacific Ocean used large stones as money. Some of their stone money was up to 12 feet (3.5 meters) in diameter and weighed hundreds or even thousands of pounds (kilograms). People used blocks of tea as money in China, Tibet, and Siberia, while Ethiopians used blocks of salt. Some American Indian money was made of shell beads called wampum. In the colony of Virginia, people used tobacco to pay taxes, salaries, fines, and debts.

of banks and bankers. People who were skilled at math helped keep track of financial transactions, and the field of accounting was born. Eventually, people started arguing about money. This sparked a need for courts and lawyers.

Today there are hundreds of different kinds of jobs, ranging from astronauts to zookeepers. New jobs are being created constantly.

During the Middle Ages, moneylenders were considered a
necessary evil.

THE WORLD OF MONEY

Settlers in colonial America used money from other countries, including English pounds, Spanish pesos (known as "pieces of eight"), and Dutch guilders. The United States adopted the dollar as its basic unit of money in 1792, when the country was already sixteen years old. The word *dollar* comes from *thaler*, a kind of coin first made in the 1500s in Bohemia (what is now the Czech Republic). There are many theories about the dollar sign ($). One idea is that it evolved from the number 8, representing the Spanish "piece of eight."

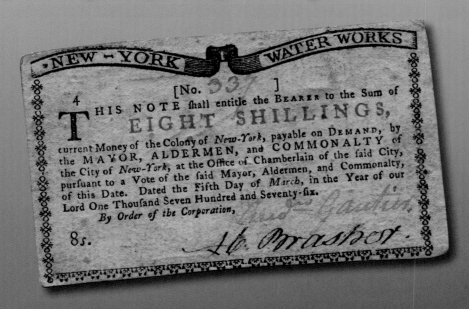

For example, in the 1730s, when George Washington was a boy, there were no professional athletes. Before the Wright brothers flew their first airplane in the early 1900s, there was no such thing as a pilot. Today, professional athletes and jet pilots are among the highest-paid professionals. The modern computer was not invented until the mid-1900s. Today, millions of people work in jobs that involve computers. Many years from now, people will have jobs that we cannot even imagine.

Construction workers frame a house. The number of new homes under construction is an important indicator of a nation's economic strength.

THREE

WHY MUST PEOPLE EARN MONEY?

In today's world, almost everything costs money. The single largest expense for most families is their home. As of 2010, the average sale price of a new home in the United States was $250,000—a quarter of a million dollars. Even people who can build their own homes need to spend many thousands of dollars on lumber, bricks, nails, and other supplies. They also have to pay for the land itself.

Now that fewer Americans are farmers, food has become a major expense. The typical American family of four spends about $10,000 a year on food—about $2,500 per person.

Another large expense is transportation. The average American household spends about $10,000 a year going from place to place. This includes the cost of gasoline, upkeep of a car, and use of public transportation.

Next to buying a house, one of today's biggest family expenses is a college education. A single year of college can cost between $12,000 and $50,000. For a four-year college education, that amounts to between $48,000 and $200,000.

Taxes are a huge expense for most Americans. The typical American household pays about $30,000 per year in taxes. The biggest chunk is income tax, which goes to the federal government. People also pay property taxes and a variety of state and local taxes.

The list of expenses goes on and on. Americans spend a fortune on health care and health insurance. And what about *fun*? A vacation for a family of four can cost several thousand dollars. As of 2010, it cost a family of four an average of $200 to attend a Major League Baseball game. In 2010, just going to a movie cost an average of $8.50 per ticket, or about $35 for a family of four—not including popcorn and drinks.

How do people find the money to pay for all these expenses? They get a job! The money that a person earns for his or her job is called a salary.

Students often take out loans and get jobs during semester breaks to help pay for their college tuition.

Here is a list of more than seventy occupations, along with the average salary for each:

OCCUPATION	AVERAGE	YEARLY	SALARY
accountant	$61,000	computer programmer	$70,000
advertising professional	$51,000	construction worker	$30,000
air traffic controller	$110,000	crossing guard	$22,000
airline pilot	$140,000	dentist	$141,000
ambulance driver	$22,000	editor	$53,000
anesthesiologist	$184,000	elementary school teacher	$49,000
architect	$70,000	emergency medical technician or paramedic	$29,000
astronomer	$95,000	family physician	$150,000
athlete (professional)	$74,000	farmer or rancher	$44,000
baker	$24,000	fashion designer	$69,000
barber	$27,000	fast-food cook	$16,000
bicycle repairer	$23,000	firefighter	$42,000
bus driver	$33,000	flight attendant	$56,000
carpenter	$40,000	forest or conservation worker	$25,000
cashier	$18,000	hairdresser	$25,000
chef	$38,000	high school teacher	$51,000
child care worker	$19,000	insurance agent	$58,000
clergy member	$43,000	interior designer	$48,000
college teacher	$72,000	custodian	$22,000
computer operator	$35,000		

judge	$96,000	radio or TV announcer	$36,000
kindergarten teacher	$47,000	real estate agent	$54,000
lawyer	$114,000	registered nurse	$60,000
librarian	$51,000	reporter	$42,000
locomotive engineer	$62,000	salesperson	$34,000
manicurist or pedicurist	$21,000	secretary	$28,000
middle school teacher	$49,000	surgeon	$184,000
music composer or director	$53,000	tailor or dressmaker	$25,000
orthodontist	$177,000	taxi driver or chauffeur	$22,000
painter, sculptor, or illustrator	$47,000	truck driver	$36,000
pediatrician	$141,000	umpire or sports referee	$27,000
pharmacist	$94,000	usher	$18,000
photographer	$32,000	veterinarian	$81,000
physicist	$96,000	waiter or waitress	$17,000
police officer	$48,000	word processor	$31,000
postal service letter carrier	$44,000	writer or author	$58,000
preschool teacher	$26,000	zoologist or wildlife biologist	$56,000
private detective	$38,000		

(Source: U.S. Department of Labor)

MOMS WHO DON'T WORK

In 2010, a website called salary.com estimated that the yearly dollar value of a stay-at-home mother was $122,611. This estimate took into account the money that her husband would otherwise have to pay for the services she provides: child care, cooking, cleaning, and tutoring the children. However, this estimate does not take into account sleepless nights spent with a sick child, hours spent shopping, or time spent looking after older relatives. The U.S. Bureau of Labor Statistics placed a lower value on a stay-at-home mom's work: about $79,000 per year.

Until recently, women were a fairly small part of the U.S. workforce. As recently as 1950, only 29 percent of American women worked outside the home. The man was the "breadwinner" in most households. Today, however, about 75 percent of American women have jobs outside the home. This change happened partly because it has become so difficult for a family to make ends meet. It also happened because job opportunities for women grew dramatically.

Earning money is probably the main reason why people work. As you will see in the next chapter, though, it is not the only reason.

Whether it involves producing bread, bricks, or Buicks, a great job combines a pleasant work environment and an enjoyable skill or service that others value.

"CHOOSE A JOB YOU LOVE"

About 2,500 years ago, an ancient Chinese philosopher named Confucius said, "Choose a job you love, and you will never have to work a day in your life." He meant that people who enjoy their jobs feel like they are having fun rather than working. The average American adult works roughly forty hours a week, fifty weeks out of the year. This amounts to two thousand hours of work per year—an awful lot of time to spend doing something you do not like! Yet millions of people are in that situation. According to a 2006 survey, slightly more than half of American workers are unhappy with their jobs.

JOB OR CAREER?

A career is the kind of work a person does, such as nursing or education. A job is the specific title for the work that a person does.

When choosing a career path, you may face a tough decision: Should you get a job that will definitely earn you a lot of money, or should you get a job that you like, even if you might make very little money? Let's talk about two young people we'll call Tony and Marie.

From the time he was in sixth grade, Tony has dreamed of becoming a professional basketball player. However, his family wants him to become a lawyer. Tony's relatives point out that very few basketball players make it to the pros. Tony, now twenty years old, knows that becoming a professional basketball player is a long shot. Yet he loves the sport, and he feels that he will always regret it unless he gives it a try. To complicate matters, Tony and his girlfriend plan to get married soon. It will be important for him to have a reliable income.

Marie has always been fascinated by the ocean, and she loves taking pictures. Now eighteen years old, she wants to become an undersea photographer. Her parents are against the idea. They think taking pictures deep in the ocean is dangerous. They have also read

Some jobs lead to exotic locations like this one in the Surin Islands off Thailand's coast, but most involve a commute of less than an hour's drive from home.

that the average photographer earns just $32,000 a year. Marie is a brilliant student, and she is especially good at science. Her parents want her to become a physician—a career that might earn her five times the income she would make photographing fish. Her parents have even offered to pay for medical school, but Marie would have to pay her own way through college if she studies photography.

The automotive industry is an important component of the U.S. economy. Even when new car sales stall, replacement parts like these exhaust pipes are needed to keep older cars running.

What should Tony and Marie do? There are no easy answers for our two make-believe young people. The most important thing is that they make their own career choices. Many family relationships have been destroyed because young people felt pressured to choose certain careers and ended up resenting their families.

There are other important factors to consider when choosing a career. Is the profession popular, or is it fading out? People who went into the horse-and-buggy business around the year 1900 soon discovered that it was the wrong choice. On the other hand, people who entered the automobile business became part of a growing industry. Even booming industries change over time. During the recession of 2008 and 2009, tens of thousands of people in the auto-making industry lost their jobs. According to the U.S. Department of Labor, "hot," high-paying jobs for 2010 to 2014 will include registered nurses and college teachers.

You should also ask yourself this question: Is your chosen job likely to grow, both in salary and in work that challenges you? As the years pass, the cost of living rises. Goods that sold for $10 in 1915 cost $30 in 1960, $130 in 1990, and $220 in 2010. These price increases over time are known as inflation. Inflation steadily increases the cost of goods and decreases the buying power of money. To keep up with inflation, an employer must offer salary increases, or raises.

HEALTH INSURANCE

A day in the hospital can cost thousands of dollars. People use health insurance to help pay for hospital stays and other medical treatment. Workers and/or their employers pay fees to an insurance company. In return, the insurance company pays for all or part of the person's medical care. For many employees, the portion they pay for their health insurance is taken out of their paychecks.

Generally, the jobs that pay the most to start with have the most potential for big raises. In nearly every industry, some companies offer raises and bonuses (extra payments) for a job well done.

Here is another important question: Should you go into business for yourself, or should you work for somebody else? A hairdresser, for instance, might work for an established salon. On the other hand, he might set up his own salon and hire other hairdressers to work for him. A writer, illustrator, or photographer might work full-time for a magazine, newspaper, or book publisher. Or she might become a freelancer, which means that she works for herself and completes projects for several different people or companies, called clients.

Working for an established company and working for yourself both have advantages and drawbacks. It is usually considered less risky to work for someone else. On the other hand, people who are self-employed usually have more freedom and independence than those workers who must report to a boss. But their career is more risky, because they do not have a guaranteed, regular salary. No worker is completely safe, though. During the 2008 and 2009 recession, companies fired thousands of lawyers. Thousands of photographers, artists, and writers who thought they had secure jobs got fired as well. As for self-employed people, instead of feeling independent, many of them complained about the cost of health insurance and high taxes.

Finally, when you are considering jobs, ask about the employee benefits, or extra resources, that come with it. Some jobs come with medical and dental insurance. These are very precious benefits because health insurance is expensive to pay for on your own. Some firms offer stock—a piece of ownership in the company—which can be extremely valuable if the company does well. Vacation time is another important benefit. For example, although teaching is not the highest-paid profession, most teachers have about fourteen weeks of vacation each year. They can use this time to travel, to enjoy their hobbies, or even to work at a second job.

A chocolate chef supervises a student. Specialty schools train people for careers as diverse as computer programming, homeland security, and massage therapy.

FIVE

PREPARING FOR THE WORKING WORLD

There is no certain way to get a dream job or to earn megabucks. However, a college education increases the chances of reaching your career goals. Many desirable careers require a college education or special schooling. These careers include doctors, lawyers, teachers, dentists, pharmacists, librarians, registered nurses, and veterinarians.

There are some stories of self-made millionaires and even billionaires who never completed college. For example, Bill Gates dropped out of Harvard University to start his own business, which became the giant Microsoft Corporation. As of 2010, Gates was the world's wealthiest person, with a total fortune of $40 billion.

However, we can't all be like Bill Gates. Studies have proven that a college degree generally increases your chances of earning a good living. According to the U.S. Census Bureau, a worker with only a high school diploma can expect to earn $1.2 million over the course of his or her career. This amounts to $27,000 per year of work. Someone with a college education can expect to earn $2.1 million, or $48,000 per working year. People with doctoral and professional degrees earn an average of $4 million over their careers, which comes out to $91,000 per year of work.

Although most college students choose a major—one area of study, such as biology or history—it is also wise to study a variety of subjects in college. A young woman we'll call Anna wanted to become a middle school science teacher. In her small hometown, however, the only job opening in the middle school was for a history teacher. Fortunately, Anna took a few history courses in college, and she got the job.

Bill Gates is chairman of Microsoft and also heads a charitable organization, the Bill and Melinda Gates Foundation, which focuses on education, health care, and poverty issues worldwide.

KIDS AT WORK

Children can earn money, just like adults. Many young people receive an allowance in exchange for setting the table, taking out the garbage, or doing other chores. In the summertime, many children set up lemonade stands. Young people also earn money by establishing neighborhood dog-walking, lawn-mowing, leaf-raking, and snow-shoveling services. However, laws protect children by restricting the amount of work they can do.

U.S. child labor laws permit teens fourteen to fifteen years old to work in certain nonhazardous jobs, such as in retail and food establishments, for three hours on school days and eight hours on nonschool days.

Ben is another example of how getting a broad education can be helpful in the working world. Ben dreamed of becoming a novelist. He majored in creative writing in college, but he also took journalism and TV broadcasting courses. Ben still hasn't sold his first novel, but he earns a good living and enjoys his work as a newspaper writer and host of a local TV show.

There are lots of myths about many jobs. For example, many people think that astronomers stay up all night and gaze at stars. Actually, astronomers are more often sitting at their computers and solving math problems. You may think that professional athletes work only a few hours per day or even per week. Actually, when they are not playing a game, pro athletes are working hard on the practice field or in the weight room. It is smart to get beyond the myths. Learn all you can about a job before preparing for it. If you want to become a pharmacist, speak to a pharmacist or observe her at work. If you want to work with young children, volunteer at a nursery school.

Looking for a job in the classified ads in newspapers is a start, but going online and checking a company's website or other employment sites is more productive.

SIX

HOW DO YOU FIND A JOB?

One common way of finding a job is to look in the newspaper. You'll see job openings in a section of the paper called the want ads, or the classified ads. A want ad describes a few basic facts about a job and tells readers how to apply for the position.

The Internet is a fantastic source for finding a job. Many companies list available jobs on their websites. You can also use a search engine to look for the kind of job you want. For example, one job seeker found 382,000 websites when she did an Internet search for "teaching jobs Chicago Illinois area" and 212,000 sites for "nursing jobs New Orleans Louisiana area." Many of the listings are repeats or otherwise unhelpful, but that still leaves plenty of possibilities.

Networking at a job fair. Employers are focused on quickly
evaluating dozens of candidates, so it's important to be prepared
to market yourself during several brief (30-second to 3-minute)
interviews at the event.

Some job hunters register with employment agencies. These are companies that match workers with jobs. Many employment agencies charge money for their services. For example, in return for finding a person a job, an employment agency receives a portion of the person's salary for a certain length of time.

Cities sometimes hold job fairs—big events where job seekers and employers meet face-to-face. Job fairs for teachers are popular. At these events, future teachers meet with school leaders.

Statistics show that networking is the number-one way to find a job. Networking means talking to as many people as you can about something that you want to do—in this case, getting a job. In fact, at least 60 percent of jobs are filled through networking. What does this mean for you? It means that when you want a job, announce it to everyone you know and everyone you meet. Spread the word!

For example, suppose you want to get a job with an advertising company. You go to your uncle's house for a barbecue. When someone asks you how life is going, you tell everyone that you are looking for a job in advertising. You do the same thing at a neighborhood picnic and at your friend's wedding. You never know. Someone you meet may be the head of an advertising company looking for bright young employees—or might know of such a person.

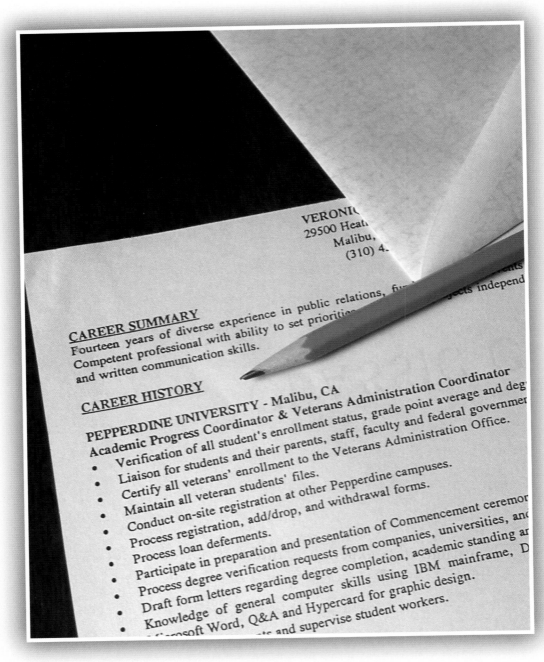

CAREER SUMMARY
Fourteen years of diverse experience in public relations, fun
Competent professional with ability to set priori
and written communication skills.

CAREER HISTORY
PEPPERDINE UNIVERSITY - Malibu, CA
Academic Progress Coordinator & Veterans Administration Coordinator

- Verification of all student's enrollment status, grade point average and deg
- Liaison for students and their parents, staff, faculty and federal governmer
- Certify all veterans' enrollment to the Veterans Administration Office.
- Maintain all veteran students' files.
- Conduct on-site registration at other Pepperdine campuses.
- Process registration, add/drop, and withdrawal forms.
- Process loan deferments.
- Participate in preparation and presentation of Commencement ceremon
- Process degree verification requests from companies, universities, and
- Draft form letters regarding degree completion, academic standing ar
- Knowledge of general computer skills using IBM mainframe, D
  Microsoft Word, Q&A and Hypercard for graphic design.
  and supervise student workers.

VERONIC
29500 Heat
Malibu,
(310) 4

Some people hire professional "resumé doctors" to help them write and
format a document that will lead to more interviews and better job offers.

SEVEN

LANDING THE JOB

Now that you've searched for a job and found some possibilities, how do you actually land the job you want? First, contact the company or person by telephone, letter, or e-mail. The employer might send an application for you to fill out. You will also be expected to send a copy of your resumé. A resumé is a one-page summary of your education, work experience, interests, job qualifications, and career goals. Think of your resumé as a fact sheet, autobiography, and advertisement for *you*.

Employers often sift through large piles of resumés. For this reason, it is vital that your resumé be well written and organized, and that it highlight your strengths. For help with writing your resumé, look for guidebooks at the library and tips on the Internet.

Job seekers should have dozens of copies of their resumé on hand, because many possible employers may request to see it. You can also post your resumé online, so a potential employer can get to it with the click of a mouse.

If an employer thinks you seem right for a job, he or she will probably invite you to come in for an interview. The interviewer may be the head of the company or a company official. An interview is usually the most important part of applying for a job. Interviewers usually ask applicants questions like these:

- How did you find out about this job?

- Why do you feel you are a good fit for this job?

- What are your strengths as an employee?

- How do you handle challenges on the job?

When you go on a job interview, it's important to make a good impression. Wear appropriate, neat clothing. Arrive at the interview a little early. Be friendly, and introduce yourself to everyone you meet at the place of business. Address the interviewer respectfully. Speak clearly and with correct grammar, as if you are talking to your English teacher. Bring paper and a pen so that you can take notes. Always answer questions honestly—most interviewers can tell if you are avoiding the truth. Finally, do not worry if you're nervous. Nervousness just means that you care, and it might actually impress an interviewer.

"Nothing great was ever achieved without enthusiasm," wrote the American essayist Ralph Waldo Emerson. If there is one quality a job candidate should show at an interview, it is enthusiasm. Employers want to hire people who are enthusiastic.

An interview is an opportunity for you, the applicant, to ask questions, too. Here are some examples: What will I do on the job? Who will be my manager? About how much will the salary be? Will there be opportunities for more challenging positions in the future? Ask questions that show your genuine interest in the job.

Following the interview, send your interviewer a thank-you note. Thank him or her for considering you for the job. Besides being polite, a thank-you note keeps you fresh in the interviewer's mind.

Make direct eye contact during the interview, and ask questions that indicate you have done research into the company.

Keep in mind that finding a job usually takes time. Only a fortunate few land a job after a single interview with one company. You will probably send out dozens of applications and resumés, and then go to dozens of interviews, before someone offers you a job. Don't be disappointed if your first job offer takes a few months.

A positive attitude is key, especially when working with the public.

LIFE ON A JOB

EIGHT

Your job quest has ended, and you have become an employee. Now it is time to begin earning a living.

Job counselors offer these simple tips for success on a job. First, be on time. Everyone is late once in a while, due to illness, traffic jams, and personal emergencies. Still an employee should be on time or early nearly every day. Also, don't bolt out the door the moment your workday has ended. In fact, if you are in the middle of a task at the end of the day, you might consider staying a few extra minutes to complete it. Bosses appreciate employees who show more interest in their work than in the clock.

Job counselors also advise people to be friendly and polite to the people they work with. It is not hard to say hello and exchange a few friendly words with your co-workers. Think of it this way: One day the person at the next desk may be your boss. He or she will remember co-workers who were friendly long before they had anything to gain by it.

Here are some other tips for success on the job:

- Do not make personal phone calls during business hours.

- Do not use office computers to send personal messages or to surf the Internet.

- Always be prepared to share your ideas and listen to others' ideas at meetings.

- Work hard, but do not overwork. Working too hard can lead to burnout and illness.

There is hardly any job where people work totally alone. It is common for any group to include some people who do not get along. Smart employees avoid taking sides in office battles. Keep your focus on your work, not on office gossip.

WISE OLD SAYINGS

English: 'Tis money that begets money.
Yiddish: With money in your pocket, you are wise and you are handsome and you sing well, too.
Mauritanian (Africa): He who loves money must labor.
Japanese: Money grows on the tree of persistence.

There is another old saying that "Money doesn't grow on trees."

Actually, it does in one way. There is a plant called a money tree that is reputed to attract wealth. Money trees have a lot of green stuff—leaves. There are also plants called dollar weeds, whose green leaves resemble silver dollars. Dollar weeds are in the parsley family. Some people add the plant's leaves to salads.

A "team player" is an asset to any company.

SOCIAL SECURITY

Social Security is a U.S. government program that provides income for elderly and retired people. The amount people receive is based on the amount they contributed through Social Security taxes when they had jobs.

What about the money? Some people, such as doctors, dentists, and veterinarians, receive payments for their services every day. Many others receive a paycheck every week or every other week. Although some workers are paid by check, many people have their wages deposited into their bank accounts electronically. This is called direct deposit.

When they see their first paycheck, people new to the workforce are often surprised when the amount is lower than they expected. You'll see this lower amount because federal and state taxes and Social Security are deducted from, or taken out of, each paycheck. Money may also be deducted for a portion of your health insurance.

Self-employed people pay more for taxes and health care than people who work for someone else. This is because employers often pay part of these costs for their employees. People who work for themselves must pay the entire amount.

Despite all the deductions, receiving your first paycheck is a special thrill. It marks the beginning of earning a living, and it gets you dreaming about promotions and bigger paychecks in the years ahead.

WHAT ARE TAXES FOR?

Federal income taxes go to the Internal Revenue Service, which collects money for the U.S. government. The U.S. government uses the money to pay for expenses such as the military, salaries of U.S. government workers, Social Security and other federal programs, and the U.S. space program. As of 2010, every state except Alaska, Florida, Nevada, South Dakota, Texas, Washington, and Wyoming had a state income tax. This money pays for the salaries of state government workers, state roads, schools, and other expenses. States without an income tax find other ways to fund their services, such as a sales tax.

GLOSSARY

apply — To try to get something, such as a job.

barter — To trade or exchange one thing for another.

career — The kind of work a person does, such as fashion designing or real estate.

clients — People or organizations that use the services of other people or organizations.

cost of living — The amount of money needed to buy basic goods and services.

currency — Another word for money.

deducted — Subtracted or taken away.

employee benefits — Items such as health insurance that employees may receive in addition to their salaries.

employee — A person who works for another person or company for pay.

employer — A person or business that pays a person or group of people to work.

expense — Money spent to buy or do something.

fertile — Able to produce something.

financial — Relating to money.

freelancer — A self-employed person who does services for other people or companies.

income tax — A tax on a person's income (money received for work).

industry — A branch of business, trade, or manufacturing.

inflation — The increase in the cost of goods and services over time.

jobs — Titles for the specific work people do either for an employer or on their own.

networking — The informal process of spreading the word about something a person wants to achieve, such as finding a job.

occupations — Activities at which people earn a living.

philosopher — A person who studies the basic nature of reality, matter, nature, and life.

professional — Trained to earn money for a specific activity or job.

qualifications — Traits or skills that make a person fit for a job.

recession — A period when the economy suffers more losses than gains. Large numbers of jobs are lost, and business activity is reduced.

resumé — A one-page summary of a person's education, work experience, interests, job qualifications, and career goals.

salary — Pay for doing a job, usually over an entire year.

self-employed — Working for oneself.

transaction — A deal or exchange of goods.

transportation — The act of moving things or people from place to place.

FURTHER INFORMATION

Blatt, Jessica. *The Teen Girl's Gotta-Have-It Guide to Money*. New York: Watson-Guptill Publications, 2008.

Brancato, Robin F. *Money: Getting It, Using It, and Avoiding the Traps: The Ultimate Teen Guide*. Lanham, MD: The Scarecrow Press, 2007.

Deering, Kathryn R., ed. *Cash and Credit Information for Teens: Tips for a Successful Financial Life*. Detroit: Omnigraphics, 2005.

Murphy, Patricia J. *Earning Money: How Economics Works*. Minneapolis: Lerner Publishing, 2006.

Orr, Tamra. *A Kid's Guide to Earning Money*. Hockessin, DE: Mitchell Lane Publishers, 2009.

WEBSITES

You can find lots of money tips on this U.S. government website:

www.kids.gov/6_8/6_8_money_earning.shtml

On this website you will find a list of jobs kids can do, tips for success, and suggested fees for each task:

www.kidsmoney.org/makemone.htm

Here are ten ways a thirteen-year-old can earn money:

www.associatedcontent.com/article/1533217/ten_ways_that_ thirteen_year_old_kids.html?cat=9

BIBLIOGRAPHY

Beam, Linda J. *The Geek's Guide to Job Hunting*. Birmingham, AL: Crane Hill Publishers, 2006.

Frisch, Carlienne A. *Everything You Need to Know About Getting a Job*. New York: Rosen Publishing Group, 2000.

Hall, Alvin, with Karl Weber. *You and Your Money: It's More Than Just the Numbers*. New York: Atria Books, 2007.

Holloway, Diane, and Nancy Bishop. *Before You Say "I Quit!": A Guide to Making Successful Job Transitions*. New York: Collier Books, 1990.

Ivey, Allison. *The Geek's Guide to Personal Finance*. Birmingham, AL: Crane Hill Publishers, 2006.

Savage, Terry. *The Savage Truth on Money*. New York: John Wiley & Sons, 1999.

INDEX

INDEX

Dennis and Judy Fradin are the authors of more than 150 books. They co-author many of their books, but in some cases Dennis writes the text and Judy obtains the pictures. The Fradins first became known for their fifty-two-book series about the states, *From Sea to Shining Sea*, which they did for Children's Press. Their first series for Marshall Cavendish Benchmark was *Turning Points in U.S. History*.

In recent years the Fradins have written many award-winning books about the Underground Railroad, early American history, and great but underappreciated women. Their Clarion book *The Power of One: Daisy Bates and the Little Rock Nine* was named a Golden Kite Honor Book. Another of their Clarion books, *Jane Addams: Champion of Democracy* won the Society of Midland Authors Best Children's Nonfiction Book of the Year Award.

Currently the Fradins are working on several projects, including a picture book about a slave escape for Walker and a book on *Tornadoes* for National Geographic Children's Books. In addition, Dennis is writing the text and Judy is obtaining the pictures for *Kids Who Overcame*, a book about young people who overcame handicaps to achieve something noteworthy.

The Fradins have three grown children and six grandchildren. In their free time, Judy is a passionate gardener with a special love for dahlias, and Dennis is an amateur astronomer and huge baseball fan.